BOOK AN

Written by El
Translated by C

No and Me

BY DELPHINE DE VIGAN

Bright
≡**Summaries**.com

DELPHINE DE VIGAN

FRENCH NOVELIST

- **Born in 1966 in Boulogne-Billancourt**
- **Selected works:**
  - *No and Me* (2007), novel
  - *Underground Time* (2009), novel
  - *Nothing Holds Back the Night* (2011), novel

Delphine de Vigan was born in 1966 in the region of Paris. In 2001, she became well-known for her autobiographical novel on the topic of anorexia, *Days Without Hunger*, published under the pseudonym Lou Delvig. The collection of short stories *The Pretty Boys* (2005) and the novel *One Evening in December* (2005) have love as a main theme and have been very well received by readers. In 2008, she received the Prix des Libraires for her bestseller *No and Me* (2007) and the Prix Renaudot des Lycéens for *Nothing Holds Back the Night* (2011).

NO AND ME

THE MOVING TALE OF AN UNLIKELY FRIENDSHIP

- **Genre:** Novel
- **Reference edition:** *No et moi*, Paris, JC Lattès, 2008, 285 p.[1]
- **1st edition:** 2007
- **Themes:** friendship, mutual aid, difference, poverty, homelessness

No and Me (2007), transposed to the screen in 2010, is a first-person story about a gifted preadolescent girl aged 13, Lou Bertignac. She reveals her questions about life, about her family and human relations, about love and, above all, about human misery. Lou meets an 18-year-old homeless girl, No, whom she helps to overcome her situation. A true friendship develops between the two girls. The story is both simple and touching. The author's talent lies especially in the description of the girl's emotions, moods, hopes, disillusions and learning. *No and Me* is a life lesson that combines social and personal aspects.

---

[1] Quotes taken from the reference edition have been translated by BrightSummaries.com.

SUMMARY

THE MEETING

At Austerlitz station in Paris, a young girl, Lou Bertignac, meets a young homeless girl, Nolwenn, who is known as No. She immediately decides that the object of her project for her economic and social science class will be homelessness. "I will document the journey of a young homeless woman" (p. 12-13), she announces. She does not foresee the changes that will happen in her own life after this meeting.

To prepare her project, the girl invites No for a drink, in order to discuss her life path, but at first No prefers to listen to Lou. During their various meetings, Lou learns that the young girl is 18, that she has been living on the streets for a few months, and that she is sometimes offered shelter by acquaintances. Lou fills an entire notebook with No's experiences and, in order to prepare for her school project, conducts research on the homeless.

During one of their meetings, Lou notices that No is beautiful despite the black marks and dirty hair. Back at home, she remembers every word of her discussion with No. During dinner, her father is, as usual, very animated, but this time Lou does not join in with the conversation. She is very affected by her mother's indifference, who has been depressed for a few years following the death of Lou's sister.

THE PROJECT

When the young girl presents her project, her classmates applaud and she receives a mark of 18/20. Lou then returns to the station to tell No about her success, but she isn't there. The saleswoman of a newspaper stand who knows the homeless girl explains that she hasn't been back for quite some time. She adds that Lou should end her friendship with the homeless girl: the worlds they live in are completely different.

The young girl goes to a supermarket where an old friend of No works, in order to ask about the girl, but the person doesn't know anything. Lou then goes to look for her in a street where a homeless person sometimes used to offer No shelter: the man tells her she might find her in a soup kitchen. Lou actually finds No a few days later, queuing up to receive her ticket. But she pushes her away violently: "I don't need you" (p. 102), "Clear off [...] it's not your life, get it? It's not your life." (p. 103). Lost and angry at No, Lou leaves: "She and all the homeless people on earth, they just have to be more friendly, less dirty, and that's it. They just have to make the effort to be nice instead of drinking on benches and spitting." (p. 104).

LUCAS

One day, Lou is surprised to see No in front of her school. She invites her to eat. No tells her that she is in an emergency shelter and is looking for work, but because she doesn't have an address, no one wants to hire her. Lou in turn confesses her feelings for Lucas, one of her friends. After the holidays, Lucas joined her on the bus to school and asked to take her to the skating rink. Lou is thrilled that Lucas, who she finds incredibly handsome, prefers to stay with her instead of with the other girls. She asks No how to kiss a boy, which makes the girl laugh. No makes vague allusions to her relationship with an unknown boy called Loïc.

So that No can have an address and therefore find work, Lou has the idea that she can live in her home. She manages to convince her parents. In the beginning, No sleeps a lot and always tells Lou:

"We're in this together." (p. 136). She gets on well with Lou's mother, whom she confides in about her origins and helps with the housework. As for Lucas, he often invites the two girls to his house and, at school, spends lots of time with Lou.

No is finally taken on as a housekeeper in a hotel. The work is hard and she becomes nervous, sometimes taking her feelings out on Lou. One day, she wants to go and visit her mother, who lives in subsidized housing; Lou goes with her. But when No knocks on the door, and even though she insists and gets angry, her mother does not answer.

Soon after, the Bertignacs leave for a few days for Dordogne. When they return to Paris, they notice a change: No, who works nights, is drinking a lot of alcohol, leaving her things lying around and isn't showing up to the meetings with her social worker. Yet, if she wants to stay in their home, she must respect their life, as Lou's father explains to No. No then takes refuge at Lucas' house.

NO'S DISAPPEARANCE

Lucas decides, along with Lou, to look after No without anyone knowing. No begins to save money: she wants to join her friend Loïc, who works in Ireland. However, she continues to drink, which affects Lucas: because of her, he arrives to school late and doesn't do his homework. No also acquires a lot of money and won't say where she got it from.

When Lou's parents find out what their daughter has been doing, they warn Lucas' mother. No is forced to leave and Lou wants to leave everything and go with her to Ireland. Before No leaves, the two girls spend the day walking to the cinema and in bistros, and No buys all sorts of things for Lou. In the morning, after spending the night in a shabby hotel, they go to Saint-Lazare station to buy tickets to England, where they will then take the ferry to Ireland. No, who wants to buy the tickets herself, asks Lou to wait for her. But a few hours later, she still hasn't come back.

Lou then goes home and reassures her parents. With Lucas, she goes to see No's old friend who works in the supermarket: she has no news of No and reveals that Loïc was never in a relationship with her, despite what No claimed. One day, by surprise, Lucas takes Lou's face in his hands and kisses her.

CHARACTER STUDY

LOU BERTIGNAC

Lou is a young, intellectually precocious 13-year-old girl. She skipped two grades at school, so she is the smallest and youngest in her class. Her father encourages her to develop her intellectual curiosity: he offers her encyclopedias which she devours. After the onset of the mother's depression, she had been enrolled into a school for the gifted in Nanterre and she only returned home once every two weeks. Each time she left for Nanterre, she hoped that "one day [her father] would put his foot down on the accelerator [...] throwing all three of them into the wall of the car park, united forever" (p. 59). It is at this moment that her feelings of loneliness began to grow.

This is the feeling that pushes her to cling to No's destiny. No's daily life is felt by Lou like "a gift that weighs heavily [...], a gift that changes the colors in the world, a gift that calls into question all theories" (p. 75). She then does all she can to save No. Having someone to call on and not being alone anymore "makes a difference" (p. 238) for No, but also for Lou. The young girl cannot accept that human beings live in worlds separated on the basis of arbitrary criteria such as money or power. She wants the worlds to "communicate with each other" (p. 86). By helping No and becoming her friend, she wants to reconcile the two opposing worlds.

Lou doesn't like speaking in public because she feels like she cannot master the power of words and prefers to keep to herself the "excess, abundance, these words that [she] [...] multiplies in silence to approach the truth" (p. 30). Even though she is not very communicative with her friends, nor with her parents, deep down inside she is very active. She is constantly thinking, counting things, drawing parallels and comparisons, and observing. For example, she wonders how it is possible to go to the moon and at the same time let homeless people die on the streets, or when she smells cabbage, she begins to list all the varieties of cabbage in her head. "I always have to take the back roads and wander. It's annoying but the compulsion is stronger than me" (p. 27), she explains. She often goes to Austerlitz station because it is the ideal place for observing human emotions: "Emotion is shown by looks, gestures, movements, [...] there are all kinds of people, young, old, well-dressed, fat, thin, poorly-dressed and so on." (p. 15-16).

NO

This young 18-year-old woman is called Nolwenn. At first, she doesn't want to tell Lou much. She was actually born as the result of the rape of her mother when she was only 15 years old. Coming from a poor family, her mother had no choice but to keep the baby, but she hated her from the beginning: she could not call the baby by her name, touch her or play with her. No was raised by her grandparents, who were farmers in Brittany. When her grandmother died, No rejoined her mother, but continued to be rejected by her. Her only happy moments were when her stepfather played with her and spoke to her gently. However, he ended up leaving No's mother, who was jealous of her daughter. She then became an alcoholic and No was forced to skip school to help her. Social services eventually placed No with a foster family, where she was treated well. But as she was already a teenager with a liking for independence and dangerous experiments (alcohol, cigarettes, strange companions), she often ran away. She was then placed in a boarding school where she met Loïc, whom she fell in love with. At 18, she found herself without a diploma and with nowhere to go. She then became homeless.

When she meets Lou, she explains to her that the homeless people she speaks to are not her friends, because "outside, no one has friends". "She tells of her fear, the cold, her wandering [...] [and the] violence" (p. 68) and often interrupts her story to drink, smoke or simply be in silence. Lou interprets this as a sign of helplessness: "[Our] silence is responsible for all the helplessness of the world, our silence is like a return to the origin of things, to their truth" (p. 69).

Her experience of homelessness has made No unstable and susceptible, as can be seen when she rejects Lou, even though she is her friend. This has also made her indifferent to her own being (she spits, throws insults and gnaws at her fingernails). When she has some money, she spends it without thinking: she offers Lou a very expensive pair of sneakers and, on the eve of her departure, she treats her friend everywhere they go.

She seems convinced by the theory of the newspaper saleswoman who believes that she is not from the same world as Lou, since she cannot adapt to the Bertignac house rules. She ends up leaving her friend.

LUCAS

This 17-year-old boy, who is very handsome according to Lou and his other classmates, is not interested in school: he has already been held back twice. He has a jaded air that attracts the attention of the girls and annoys his teachers. Just like Lou and No, he suffers from loneliness: his father left his family to live in Brazil and his mother found a new partner. She rarely visits her son. Lucas therefore manages on his own. He decides to help No and he supports Lou in everything that she does. Lucas makes up stories about No's future ("of better days, luck and fairy tales") to give her courage. He is not insensitive to Lou's feelings: he understands and shares them.

ANALYSIS

A HUMANIST NOVEL

The aim of this book is not to establish itself as a social novel (since it does not take the side of one social class against another), but to highlight one of the deformities of today's society: the alarming number of homeless people and the difficulties they face in getting by. Therefore, it is more of a humanist novel, i.e. one that places man and his values above all.

What knocks in life cause people to end up on the street? Lou does not understand. For example, the homeless man that has lived in their neighborhood for years ended up on the street because when his wife left him, he couldn't handle the situation and became personally and socially lost. Other examples are given by No: "Normal women who have lost their jobs or have fled their homes, women who were beaten or driven out" (p. 72).

Homeless people, already in a very difficult situation, become even more deplorable in the long run. They cannot find work, are forced to queue for a bowl of soup, are chased out of shops as soon as they take refuge there to warm up, are dirty, etc. Prospective employers take advantage of their weak position, as is the case with No: she was hired part-time; but works full-time and, in addition to doing the housework, she must also take care of the bar and welcome guests. Moreover, there is a lot of violence amongst the homeless, as shown in the episode in the soup kitchen, where they fight for seats, or that of the two women who fight over a cigarette butt. "This is what we become, animals, fucking animals" (p. 74), explains No when telling Lou about the episode. Thus, they seem to belong to another universe, just like No thinks. When No passes, indifferently, by a homeless person who sheltered her a few times and pretends not to see him, Lou, who is accompanying her, tells her that he is still her friend. No, who has a job, then turns back and gives him 20 euros, but he refuses the cash and spits on the ground. Is he convinced, just like No, that the homeless are part of a different world to those with financial means and that, in that world, there are rules to respect, and a hierarchy or dignity that is difficult to understand?

Delphine de Vigan points to a malfunctioning in the current society, which is capable of technological progress but is unable to care for the poor. Society is becoming mechanized and dehumanized. This also seems to be Lou's conclusion. Thus, in the novel, the author denounces the rejection and stigmatization of the homeless by some of their fellowmen, who are indifferent.

Note that the author also wants to highlight the pervasiveness of violence, which is not only present among the homeless. Lou, who thought that violence was physical, discovers new forms of violence in No's silences ("violence is the time that covers injuries, [...] this impossible return", p. 261), in the lack of reaction from her mother ("my mother remains standing [...] arms down by her sides. The violence is there too, in this impossible gesture that goes from her to me, the gesture that is forever suspended") and in daily life ("One had only to count those who spoke to themselves or go awry, or had only to take the metro", p. 278). In our society, violence is everywhere.

But Lou wants to prove that looking around and opening up to others is the only thing needed to change the course of events:

> "One day we focus on a figure, on a person, we ask questions, we try to find reasons, explanations. Then we count. The others, the thousands. Like the symptom of our sick world. Things are what they are. But I believe we need to keep our eyes wide open. To begin with." (p. 79)

THEME OF SOLITUDE

The loneliness of the young people is also evident in this novel.

Lou, although loved and living in a wealthy family, feels alone and finds a friend in No, with whom she has nothing in common except the fact that they are alone. When she decides to help No and not give up on her, she leads the project alone (her parents only accept No as long as she doesn't stray). Lou knows exactly when her loneliness began: on day, after the death of her sister, when she was riding a bicycle in a park with her mother, she fell, but her mother did not see anything and did not react. It was another woman who helped her to her feet. The woman then made a sign with her hand: "A sign like this [...] means that you will have to be strong, you will have to grow up with this. Or rather, without it." (p. 244), i.e. without the affection of her mother.

No was also abandoned by her mother. Lou is under the impression that when No confides in her own mother, she is trying to find a replacement. Lou then feels angry, especially when she hears her mother telling No how her baby died (she feels betrayed by her mother once more). But No's loneliness is particularly social: she cannot create any connection with the other homeless people she knows, and the social assistance system does nothing but put more pressure on her. She builds a kind of internal defense system against everything and everyone as a result, which manifests through a certain independence: she rejects (her nickname also gives the idea of negation) any act of help or friendship. She accepts help from Lou and Lucas, but eventually leaves them.

Lucas is a particular case of loneliness. He is simply abandoned by his parents, although they love him and think they can compensate for their absence with checks. He is strong enough to overcome his loneliness and become a self-confident adult.

A STORY OF INITIATION AND LEARNING

No and Me is a story of initiation and learning in the sense that Lou, a preteen who is growing up, is immersed in the reality of life and acquires notions about human relationships and the functioning of society. She is confronted by different aspects of the world (homelessness, love and the lack of love, friendship) which influence her growth and help her to form personal opinions.

She used to be alone and then discovers friendship, which she idealizes. She thinks about the fox in *The Little Prince* by Antoine de Saint-Exupéry, and his interpretation of the verb 'to tame' that she memorized and wants to put into practice:

> "To me, you are still nothing more than a little boy who is just like a hundred thousand other little boys. And I have no need of you. And you, on your part, have no need of me. To you, I am nothing more than a fox like a hundred thousand other foxes. But if you tame me, then we shall need each other. To me, you will be unique in all the world. To you, I shall be unique in all the world..." (p. 212)

She is tamed by No and, as a result, she no longer needs to be alone because she has become her friend. No is unique to Lou. However, it is less certain that, in turn, No accepts or is waiting to be tamed: the fact that she abandons Lou and rejects her several times shows that she has reservations about the creation of a strong bond, even though she constantly feels the need to be reassured of her trust. This is not out of simple indifference, No is not a profiteer, but, as Lou guesses, it may simply be the fact that, since it is the first time in her life that someone really cares for her and wants to help, she doesn't know how to react.

Lou thus sees her friendship put to the test and, throughout the book, learns a lot about human relationships. In addition, she also discovers love through the character of Lucas.

FURTHER REFLECTION

SOME QUESTIONS TO THINK ABOUT...

- What human values are highlighted in this book?
- Is there a 'committed' approach from the author? Can we say that she criticizes the present social system?
- How would you explain Lou's feelings of loneliness?
- Three mothers are presented in this novel. Examine the way they are depicted and compare them.
- Lou is intellectually precocious. How does this influence her everyday life? Does she feel that this is useful?
- No prefers not to talk about herself at first. In your opinion, why is that?
- Imagine that you have to complete a project on the homeless. What would you say?
- *No and Me* was transposed to the screen in 2010. Compare the impact of the film (visual) and of the book (reading) on the public.
- This book has been very successful among young people. Why do you think this is?

FURTHER READING

REFERENCE EDITION

- De Vigan, D., 2008. *No et moi*, Paris, JC Lattès.

ADAPTATION

- *No and Me*, film by Zabou Breitman, with Nina Rodriguez and Julie-Marie Parmentier, 2010.

www.brightsummaries.com
ISBN ebook : 978-2-8062-7014-6
ISBN papier : 978-2-8062-7093-1
Dépôt legal : D/2015/12603/470

Cover: © Lisiane Detaille

Printed in Great Britain
by Amazon